said the Frog to the scorpion

Matthew E. Henry

Harbor Editions
Small Harbor Publishing

Cover art "Frog Battle Quilt" by C. R. Resetarits
Cover design by Allison Blevins
Book layout by Allison Blevins and Ellie Davis

Cover art sampled from Kawanabe Kyosai
Kawanabe Kyosai (Japanese, 1831-1889). Sketch, 19th century. Ink, paper, Sheet: 17
13/16 x 13 9/16 in. (45.2 x 34.5 cm). Brooklyn Museum, By exchange and
Designated Purchase Fund, 37.532 (Photo: Brooklyn Museum,
37.532_IMLS_SL2.jpg)

SAID THE FROG TO THE SCORPION
MATTHEW E. HENRY
ISBN 978-1-957248-19-6
Harbor Editions,
an imprint of Small Harbor Publishing

"I miss you more than I remember you."

—Ocean Vuong

not everything is about You.

but maybe You should stop reading now.

Contents

Don't write about race. Specifically, don't write about being Black . . .
The last thing people want to hear about is being Black. Being Black's a
curse—no offense—and nobody wants to feel cursed when they read
something they just finished paying $24.95 for. Know what I mean?
Here's one thing I've learned: when someone treats you terribly, the last
thing they want is for you to behave as if they've treated you terribly. If
I punch you in the neck, I don't want you bringing up that time I
punched you in the neck. It's your job, as the punchee, to grin and bear
it and treat me like I never did it. Make me feel good. Help me forget
the whole neck-punching adventure. It's common courtesy, really. And
that's just the same for the people who said they loved you and then
showed it not to be true as it is for the country that kidnapped you and
chopped off your left foot. Nobody wants their monstrosities brought
up. And if you should happen to do it, they'll hate you for it. Just ask
Frankenstein's monster.

—Jason Mott, *Hell of a Book*

said the Frog to the
scorpion

break-up || letter || of resignation

I care about   hope,   but
      don't think it's possible.

                             my efforts
        are not working   because
         you   haven't

                         been trying.
I think we've made progress.

                we haven't.

   there's no
question anymore.

         we   feel uncomfortable
as a   hug   without
               asking.

I understand
you can't be

     asked   not to be this way.

I need   to be free of   you.

     I'm   sorry if I've given you the impression that   I'm
not.

I.

What was the point of loving someone who only nipped at you with its sharp yellow teeth whenever you joyously shrieked because you were happy to see it?

—*The Very Persistent Gappers of Frip,*
George Saunders

hevel

I have to remind myself
you're not real. not a ghost
of someone who once was,
who now remains in-
complete. not a dream
cobbled from my subconscious
desires. you're the reflection
of a shadow cast on a sun-facing
window, obscuring all movement
within. the graspable portion
of fog and mist, here
in absent vanity.
the kiss never given,
leaving my cheek stained red.

how She reads it
an erasure of James Baldwin's "My Dungeon Shook"

I have begun this letter five times.   I keep seeing
your face,

which is   tough   dark   moody—   because
you want

no one to think you are soft.   you may be.

          your father

                    really believed

white people

exhibit a   tendency towards holiness.   you   are of another era—

part of   the late   cities of destruction.

          you can only be   what the   world calls

          a nigger.

I tell you this because

I love you.

                              please don't forget it.

"My apple trees will never get across
And eat the cones under his pines"

it's a strange comfort teaching in a town
where yard signs signal which homes hide rooms
stacked with jim crow trophies—
treasured testicles and tongues,
ears and lips from lynched men—
preserved in sun-yellowed mason jars
on regularly dusted shelves. a place where
presidential slogans and confederate flags
are considered gauche, and subtlety
is the new white supremacy. where placards
for housing discrimination, segregated schools,
and other NIMBY announcements
are barely veiled behind yearly propositions.
each ticky-tacky mansion a book
accurately judged by its cover
(despite the 40-page preface in the foyer
and its attempts to explain what's clear
as who their children are not allowed to date).
each ironic as a dinner party carefully measuring,
folding, cutting paper napkins and coasters
to prop-up a table leg three inches off balance,
to enjoy a microwaved meal at the local Chili's,
convinced they'll see it was all worth the effort.

the reckoning

CPH said, *"too many" can be as few as three*—
the magic number exposing how the trick is done,
light shifting from the blonde assistant to hands
concealed in the dark. the advertiser's golden ratio
of aggregate melanin. the progressive tipping point
where the cool is lost from chic restaurants, the polish
from AP classroom. where they no longer feel
embarrassed for confusing Eunice for Jackie
for Miki. Julio for Erik for Hugo. where "diverse"
slippery slopes to "awkward," "ghetto," "overrun," or
silent blue-eyed glances. the not flaxen straw
breaking the tolerant's back. it's a quaint thought.
but experience shows "too many" can be as few as
one.

when my colleagues hear our employer confused me with the only other Black teacher in the district

wait, there's another Black teacher?

  what the actual fuck?

    do you at least look alike?

      does he have a PhD too?

        Jesus Christ…

          you've been here for 7 years…

            I wish this surprised me.

          hasn't he been here for like five minutes?

        mother of God…

      isn't he a learning assistant?

    you look nothing alike.

  oh for fuck's sake.

we have another Black teacher?

"what i learned during Black History Month"
by billy, age 8 (or 18)

Black people were slaves
who were set free by a king
named Martin Luther, after
he had a dream about sitting
in the back of a bus with a lady
railroad conductor—she
convinced him not paying people
was wrong. also, his brother
George—a farmer who
invented peanut butter,
the gas mask & the stop light—
was so good at baseball, he played
with the white kids at school
in front of the national guard.
sadly, Martin was shot
on a wintery street in Boston,
which started the war of civil
rights, the Harlem Renaissance,
and birthed president Obama.

cryptography

it's a simple substitution cipher,
she said. just remember that A= 1
and the alphanumerics progress
from there: B= 2, C= 3, D= 4, E= 5, etc.
it's uncomplicated, she said, so long
as you remember that A= -1
(and thus B= -2, C= -3, D= -4, E= -5, etc.)
while decoding the ciphertext,
my message of great importance.
please remember that A= 1.61803399, or
sometimes A= 2.71828, unless A= 3.145926535—
φ, e, and π respectively—so there's no need
for me to explain, she said, what logically follows.

she hands me a crisp half-sheet—

13572829	6	7200	20 17 30	12 17 1
1600	13 954764500 27		13 257 12	
12 17 736 12 42	6 12	5	122 18	

—and waits.

fugue state in B minor

you'd have me sure that I am sleepwalking
beneath a liquid moon which ebbs and wanes
through corn silk stalks entwined like effigies.
acquainted with the patterns of our love,

you'd have me note how deep and dark—how lovely
the miles which keep me from sound sleep. walking
toward what little "we" remains in the waning,
I bask in affirmations—effigial

promises. if not effigies,
other fuckery mocking my steps of love—
a lumine clock marring sleep. walk
with me again. rage against the waning

of our light. fan the embers waning
before our hope is burned in effigy.
call me back or say goodbye—my love,
you could wake me from this sleepwalking.

pop quiz for March 19, 2018

definitions:

    (a.) *mechanism of death*: the chain of events
disordering the body. the dominoes
of corporeal dissolution (ex. COPD/lung failure/
asphyxiation/cessation of life). the black
blocks falling like seceding states.

    (b.) *cause of death*: the external interrupter
of normal order. the callous or unconscious
chain causer (ex. a three pack a day habit).
the smoking gun. the pale, pushing finger.

    (c.) *manner of death*: the natural or unnatural
circumstances (ex. accident, suicide, homicide
by cigarette). the blamed probabilities
of intent. the hand leading to the end of it all.

scenario:

    in Sacramento, CA, a 22-year-old Black man was shot in his
grandmother's backyard

instructions:

    given the above, match each of the following to the appropriate
definition

_____ poor street lighting
_____ the twenty (20) rounds fired at his body
_____ "broken windows theory"
_____ red-lining, poverty, and gentrification
_____ "community policing"
_____ the eight (8) rounds that entered his body
_____ the '94 crime bill
_____ exsanguination from a lacerated aorta and left ventricle
_____ "warrior cop" training
_____ the six (6) rounds he took in the back
_____ the two perforated lungs

_____ the cell phone in his hands

_____ fox "news"

_____ the one (1) round he took while he lay dying on the ground

_____ the fractured vertebrae

_____ the lack of aid rendered for five (5) minutes while he lay dying
on the ground, as he was told to cast aside the weapon he
didn't have

_____ white supremacy

_____ a mistake

when they ask for my opinion on their latest racial panic

it's like asking for casual sex
from a co-worker
or long-time friend
in the same tone
and cadence used
to procure a pencil
or solicit a piece of gum.
out the blue and
apropos of nothing
more than a flash
of desire—a fleeting
future-thought. reckless
curiosity, consequences
unconsidered.
a private expectation
made public privilege.
so unlike a polite
monday morning inquiry
about how the weekend was spent.

"never meaning no harm"

beyond realizing an ass-less Daisy
was unworthy of the acclaim,
every Black man of a certain age
has a *Dukes of Hazard* moment
when he questioned how good
those old boys could be weekly
jumping into General Lee's lap,
sliding across a confederate flag.
a what the fuck moment seeing
the familiar pattern bolting from
a social studies textbook instead
of an orange Charger. or learning
their rebel yell—that shotgun horn—
was a song about slaves preferring
bondage, getting homesick too far
from cotton fields and cracker whips.
unless this is a Yankee problem—
a recessive trait of the Great Migration,
rarely expressed by those who never left
The Field, who can still point to red
riverbeds and roots, who remember
the history of white men operating
outside the law—destructive
as moonshine or sweating dynamite.

nice white lady

after Lucille Clifton

wants our sons
wants our daughters
to hold her world
behind lips
tight as shackles
what will it cost
to buy our babies back?

nice white lady
says i want you
to walk through my halls
my fingers
in your nose
over your eyes
around your throat
call it love

says hear our stories
taste our bleached bread
release your drums
nobody understands you
until you speak like a
nice white lady

nice white lady
you have chained our sons
in the basement
of big houses
to the prows
of promised yachts
nice white lady
you have straightened our daughters'
magic curls
stolen their asses
nice white lady
what do we have to pay
to repossess our children?

what will we owe
to re-own our own at last?

Her takeaway

an erasure from Robin DiAngelo's White Fragility

people of color   discriminate against white
people,   transforms
            their prejudice
into racism.
            the impact: white   is   temporary.

people of color

pass legislation that prohibits   me   and everyone like me.

people of color   also
                                          discriminate against
other groups of color: this bias ultimately holds   down
whites.
                                          in the United States,
      whites have
                  no   power and privilege.

many whites see racism as a thing of the past.   we are well served

to acknowledge it in the present.

reality show

I keep forgetting all she wants
is a "yes, you're right dear,"
and silence before the credits roll.
to actually believe "it's all my fault
dear," without side-eyeing the camera,
cueing the canned laugh track—earnest,
authentic nodding, admitting the ineptitude
is mine.

        our grey sedan playing peekaboo
        through the garage door because
        I distracted her with my shout to stop.

        the comic misunderstanding, offending
        the in-laws, our daughter's physics teacher,
        and the HOA president, because I took her
        at her word, callously failed to read her mind.

        the first floor and basement flooding—
        foundation now sagging—because my notes
        to not use the dishwasher were only on
        the countertop, front latch, soap tray, and
        start button, instead of her vanity mirror.

after all this time, I should have known better. simply said,
"I'm sorry, I don't know what I was thinking dear"
when she left the baby face down in the tub.

when asked why I believed Her

do you remember going to Dave & Busters?
Funspot and Fun World? Canobie Lake Park
or whichever local boardwalk arcade helped
you escape the summer's melt, postponed
your required reading? do you remember the awe
of 8-bit graphics? the catching of breath during
cut scenes—flexing, cracking knuckles, shaking
and stretching arms, while eyes never left the screen?
graduating from collapsing and chasing colored dots—
Arkanoid and *PacMan*—to the unsteady scroll
of a hack-and-slay? the heady days of *Shinobi*
and *Ninja Gaiden*, *Altered Beast* and *Golden Axe*?
the arpeggiated symphony of synth and 808 beats
behind a beat-em up or run-and-gun? the sticky
sneaker squelch under *Super Contra* and *Street Fighter,*
Galaga and *Gauntlet*? gathering three friends to fight
Shredder in Konami's *TMNT*? the shoulder-crush
of a six-player *X-Men*? do you remember waiting
for an acned twenty-something to sanitize
the acidic yawn of popcorn, overpriced pizza,
and Mountain Dew from a cockpit cabinet—
the funnel cake spew from the ear-splitting roar
of *Star Wars* or *F1*, *Afterburner* or *Pole Position*?
before being replaced by rechargeable plastic,
do you remember how excitement was measured
by the metallic heft of coins in your pockets—how much
that well-worn bronze was worth? how their jiggling
granted white card access, the ability to assimilate
into other worlds where you could be anyone else?
each a 1up to obtain the high score and immortalize
your initials, proving to Them you're one of the good ones?
how—before the countdown ended—their brown bodies
were stacked like corpses on the deck to "continue . . . ?"
your trial-and-error creep toward the final boss
or a coveted kill screen? how your amusement,
your enjoyment, your everything was captured
in how many sambo danced through pale palms until
streetlights summoned you home? do you remember

how valuable you made those tokens feel?

who She is

"If she were a room to rent I would pay.
If she were a life to save I would save."
—*Anne Sexton*

Who is she, that one standing too close?

She's the one who threw my bones
to divine a future without my consent.
and built a house that was a classroom
empty of children. built a life broken
into 65-minute segments, interrupted
by static-filled announcements. built,
in the end, a ceremony rejected after
the song—a graduation with an unearned
diploma, a mail-order marriage.

Why do you sit with these little songs?

because She called to me and I attended
the way any child enters this building
of promised festivities and formalities—
the things that matter to an eager one
unaware of its compulsions, its intolerance
of truancy. I joined before learning the climate
is cold as a kiss permitted only after money
has been left on the table. so I made up a song
that wasn't true. I made up so many, many songs.

Do you ask me to measure such things?

perhaps. perhaps I want someone to take note.
to hear the songs she only pretended to enjoy
when public eyes pried the bruises on my dark skin.
spied my sorrows, the sorrows of my children.
in private, my skirtful of hell refused to hear
my tears, yet desired I scream the louder. slowly
I learned there was no safe space. no corner
of reprieve. only teachers unwilling to face the bully
for fear of his parents. the mean girls left to run amuck,

hoping time will heal their woundings. would that I could
honestly buy—if not win—her love. or at least her respect.
that I would marry my mind to, were there any mind left.

What is your torment compared to the small fate allotted each?

torment is torment is torment, no matter how passionate
the palm—the supposed love holding the scalpel
and bone-saw, the slim fingers spinning the dial
connecting current to testicles. no matter how cloying
the nicknames. how desperate the love-bombs. I have
no place. no peace. this house we share is a prison
the size of a folding tent and her back is always turned
to me. and I am not allowed to touch or comfort her—
she has achieved her proper gap, standardized a test
for how little she thinks I love. there is no scaling,
no curve. so I stick curled fists in my pockets,
shuffle these halls from bell to bell like a scolded child.

Do I know who she is? Have you named her enough?

maybe I shouldn't have put this into words.
I am probably worse for this kissing of ink to paper.
at least that's what she tells me. loudly, often.
I once calmed her raving. once hugged her out
with a song. but now there is no room in this chamber
for it, for me. no room for all the children called *mine*,
which should have been *ours*. I have walked
through this door in my dreams, in my waking.
I have placed my hands over my eyes and my mouth.
have serrated my tongue for as long as I could manage.
but, sober as The Judge, I see the song is not a life
I can live. is no law I can write. no writ I can hand down
like monogamy. no report whose grades are worthy
to bring into a home. time has condemned me *fool*.

formative assessment

Q.

how many times
can you say
it is what it is
without resentment?

A.

how many times
can you ask?

an open letter to the one who should have got away

                              . . . yet, somehow—
as the scorpion thrashed her pincers
and drowned—the frog survived,
flopped ashore, croaked himself
back to life. a week, a month later,
along the same muddy shore,
another barb-tailed arachnid
implored him for safe passage
across the stream. a ride
atop his slick, perforated back.
it's not that he doesn't remember.
it's just his nature. he never learns.

II.

Would it not, he proposed, be more prudent for them to love something that might actually love them back, something solid and reliable, something that was actually still present

—The Very Persistent Gappers of Frip,
George Saunders

sweetness

before she began, she placed the glass jar between us—
filled with fresh, golden honey—and a sizable spoon.
homemade. an amateur apiarist, she kept a ready supply.

as she began, I remembered how my mother mixed
honey with lemon, a pinch of salt. a folk remedy
for sore throats, the beginnings of a cold.

when she was through, I asked *why*. she thought
I meant the amber on the table, not the gaslighting
she called *brutal honesty*. she said it was to help me

swallow my feelings.

the gist: according to Her

an erasure poem from Ibram X. Kendi's How to Be an Antiracist

"antiracist" is   the global march of   racism.
"antiracist" is

the racist hate of white people.   to be "antiracist" is to
conflate racist people with white people.

                              racist non-whites   see
                    ordinary white people
as   victimizers.

                              people of color

                                                  enrich

          power
at the expense
of us.

when asked why I don't teach elementary school

           . . . so let me get this straight.
this white girl from the burbs—
golden curls, bonnet blue as her eyes—
breaks into the house of three Brown bears
with the confidence of the average ashley
gentrifying Brooklyn or Jamaica Plain.
while they are out bonding before breakfast,
she criticizes their cuisine, smashes their shit,
complains nothing fits her flat lack of contours,
and then, upon their confused return, flees
with a harrowing tale she's sure to share
at every dinner-party—a survivor's story,
her bravery in the face of rabid peril—
and I'm supposed to side with her?

when asked about white fragility

it's being in love—every chamber of your heart exposed
on sleeves, pant legs, shoe tops—then everything goes
to shit. after an appropriate amount of time, you go
someplace public for the post-mortem. to dissect
whether things ever were as they seemed and decide
what went wrong. whether blame can be laughed away
or buried for the next to excavate. you sit. listen. nod
and smile. say "yes" to their every complaint. gently
acknowledge the changing sides of their story. you assume
best intentions, grant generous silence, and wait. but
when you open your mouth to speak, the screaming
catches you off-guard. you're lost beneath the barrage
of accusations. how you *don't understand* and *always
over-generalize*. how events both *never happened* and
were *unintentional*. were no more their fault than
how their parents raised them. and as dishware flies
from the flipped table, you wonder if you should follow
their storming out. but you're focused on how they ignore
the blood on their hands as easily as the fork
they thrust into your upturned, pleading palm.

when asked what it's like to love Her

let me count the ways she disappoints, like
a faculty meeting where the admin
can't be bothered to convincingly lie,
and it all should've been in an email.
she's inconsistent as the moon. alters
hourly. weekly issues new missives
she'll misremember, yet hang round my neck.
I can't walk through these halls unencumbered
by false ties binding me to this brick house
on fire. love's no summer's day. it's not all.
bread nourishes, sleep's precious, and for air
I'd gladly trade the memories of her,
were it not for my children, whose small hands
I'll hold—strong as death—until in my grave.

the patron saint of suicide

after Joan Kwon Glass

> *". . . it is better for me to die than to live!"*
> *—The Book of Jonah* 4:3b

question:

where is the saint who refuses forgiveness?

answer:

in the Book of Jonah a man ran away from a God
who, when asked, *why do horrible things happen?*
answered, *they are Mine. I can do what I want
with them—even save them.* a prophet who knew God
could forgive anything. a victim who thought
such grace, such mercy, to be utter bullshit.
the assyrians wedged unsanded wood under ribs
and full body weight, sliced thin strips from thighs,
cheeks, and so amused themselves with amputations,
antebellum plantation owners of the American South
studied their zeal centuries later. Jonah'd rather die
than see them saved. and I get it.

stalked by a difficult marriage, caring for impossible
cases, afflictions swarming like white bees in
and out of my mouth . . . of the many times I contemplated
seeing my reflection from the other side of a frozen lake,
or the Basquiat beauty of speed and an apt guardrail
hovering over a sleeping bridge, none of my reasons
have ever been as noble, as honorable as his. or
as utilitarian. the greatest good for the greatest number
of his people. a Christ-figure frustrated by a big fish
and promises to pay what he had vowed. I get that too.

my first year teaching, a student said Jonah's mission
was equivalent to God sending my Black ass to hand out
Gospel tracts at a cross burning. I nodded at her profundity.
said something along the lines of *fuck that noise*
in my heart. given the choice, I too would choose the sea
for the sake of my skin—my people. I would choose—

like him—to be buried beside the ancestors who jumped
from the Master's ship. but nothing is certain. survival happens
despite our best efforts. in the end, Jonah remained
angry enough to die. but he remained.

while suffering their own afflictions—often
familial, always familiar—my students ask,
how do people survive here? when "forgive"
and "forget" are two sides of the unflipped coin
clenched in their fist. my most honest answer—
I have no idea—floods my dammed mouth
as I search their faces for something
that might be useful. instead I say—I believe—
we hold onto whatever keeps us going until
something better comes along, and then
we hold on to that. but sometimes, like them,
I would rather not.

summative assessment

Q.

    isn't there value
in symbolic change?
mission statements
re-visioned to include
the appropriate words.
aspirational policies
doled like candy
by dentists. careful
outreach to light-Brown
faces willing to drink
from recently de-signed
water fountains.
isn't lip service better
than nothing?

A.

    how many times
can you ask me
for the answer
you want to hear?

at some point

outrage—or simple self-respect—must take
over. stop playing the fool. love something
that can actually love back. something
solid. something reliable. sweetened
condensed milk. butter bread and grape jelly.
an honest apple on the desk. the right
four chords in a minor key. a blank page
and a good pen. a brace of black kittens.
an unstained note—gracious, grateful. a strange
room with familiar faces. barefoot friends,
no shoes to drop. find something consistent.
something that doesn't sharpen yellow teeth
and horns, goring another's joy. something
that sees you as *you*, not an obstacle.

jocko graves

         . . . so I reminded her
that my contract officially lists my position
as a full-time *English / language arts teacher*,
not *lawn jockey:*

         a comfortable token
         prominently placed
         on the district website,
         accomplishments lauded
         before the schoolboard
         without acknowledgment
         outside the public eye.

         a faithful groomsman—
         inoffensive
         and not to scale.

         a stable hand raised
         in dual-purpose—
         a lantern,
         a hitching-post.

         a lie based on her need
         to believe I'm willing
         to die for the love,
         the honor, of serving
         her concerns.

why She be so damn pissed at me all the time

after Lucille Clifton

she tells me to speak
but she wants me to speak
her truth—

        to place a hand
        over my mouth
        another in my back
        to control my eyes
        and brows, control
        the lines and curls
        of my lips and those
        beside my nose
        to play her scripted
        version of the show—

and I keep speaking
mine.

when asked about toxic amnesia

"just because you've forgotten doesn't mean you're forgiven."
—*Peter Gabriel*

 . . . but it can get so bad, some people
begin to believe their own bullshit, breaking Biggie's fourth
Crack Commandment. like how Bill Clinton did not inhale
or have sexual relations with that woman. how many
of Atwood's black-clad commanders believed the bed
and blood were not only for the good of Gilead, but
the world without end? it's convenient how discomforting
details can disappear, like whose stories go untold
every month in our curriculum. or how Jewish neighbors
"moved east" according to those who shared smiles
and meals for decades, but were silent when asked why
clothes and shoes and paintings and every precious thing
too heavy to cheek or carry in a hem, were left behind
the open doors. it's funny how often I think about the root
of the word *ignorance.* it's right there in front. loud
as cattle cars spewing ash and cinders. you know, she burns
receipts like unread books. our texts, emails, letters:
"forgotten." a study showed teaching children about
"crying wolf" only bred better liars. carolyn bryant,
said she "paid dearly," and was as much a victim
as Emmett Till. 50 years after his open casket, she wrote
a memoir—called it *I am more than a wolf whistle.* what?
no. I was going to leave Blanche DuBois out of this. recently
I was in a PD on student mental health. they told us never argue
when someone breaks with reality. that psychosis is a hell
of a drug—mind altering, but understandable. I'm never sure
of her excuse. which reminds me: I have an idea for a trendy
hand soap. it'd feature Pilate and Lady Macbeth on the label.
I still need to come up with a clever name and a catchy slogan
that's not so damn obvious. something about "white woman tears"
relies on the kindness of strangers—no matter the cost or
who has to pay. how could I forget "The Emperor's New Clothes"?
well, I'm no psychiatrist, but "repressed memory" seems to protect
the victim, and that's the difference. I'm just tired of the back
and forth. how she "never thought," "never said," "never did,"
in the face of so much forensic evidence, even Annie Dookhan
couldn't fuck up the conviction. I think it's just more honest to say,

she simply never was.

take your pick

there was the afternoon she accosted me in the parking lot,
desperately needing to midwife all the reasons I hadn't adopted
her fantasy—her inability to see the world in white and not.
or there was the time she complained I wasn't emotionally open
enough, then proceeded to slit my veins with her tongue, play

her fingers through the viscera, splay a palm-print turkey
with a buckled hat and declared June 19th a national holiday.
could it be when she said she couldn't imagine a life without me,
so fried chicken Wednesday became the cafeteria's weekly crisis?
or perhaps it was the professional development where we play-

acted at truth—eight hours listening to heartfelt confessions
of cancelable offenses and the ceaseless trauma of white guilt.
it could be when she rubbed my woolen head like a lamp,
possibly expecting three magic wishes—apparently unaware
that I'm not that type of negro (but it reminded me that the play's

only the thing when there's a conscious to catch. cheese needs
a willing mouse). it's probably when she said I wasn't nigger enough
to understand how my class, gender, and sexuality shielded me
from knowing "what it's really like to be persecuted"? —perspective
she gained during her graduate seminar in racial cosplay.

when asked how to avoid being seen as racist

. . . well, it's like the old joke about "Fergus
the goat-fucker." that's the punchline. he fucked
a wee goat, but laments the moniker's
accuracy more than his enjoyment
of drunken kid sodomy. I assume
it was only the one time, but something
engorged him—something a stiff pint of Guinness
roused from flaccid slumber, but didn't conceive.
even the Bible at Fergus' bedside says
the mouth speaks the heart, though I assume other
appendages follow suit. to answer
your question, those with a legitimate
worry should avoid petting zoos and farms,
or at least keep their zippers closed until
they've addressed the wooly desire within.

when asked what I learned during the "community forum" on the appropriateness of my poem

B	I	N	G	O
"... a Chi-com, psy-op plan to destroy America!"	"Critical Race Theory!"	"I haven't read it myself, but ..."	"... First Amendment rights ..."	"Back in my day ..."
"Deuteronomy 27:21 says ..."	"I don't care what the message is supposed to be ..."	"So called art ..."	"... pedophiles and groomers ..."	"I think you're all, purposely, missing the point ..."
"... see an exercise of my Second Amendment rights!"	"Since when is bestiality acceptable to teach children?!"	"I'm not a racist, but ..."	"While it's clear you're very articulate ..."	"[unintelligible] BLM ... [unintelligible] Antifa ... [unintelligible] George Soros."
"Stop teaching racism!"	"But what if the goat is consenting?"	"I DID take my meds this morning, thank you very much!"	"Leviticus 18:23 says ..."	"I'd like to apologize on behalf of ..."
"While you're clearly very educated ..."	"[inaudible mumble. racist slur.]"	"My rights as a parent ..."	"Please believe we're not all like this ..."	"Officers, could you please ..."

when asked why I won't

*"Does trying only count if someone else
deems your effort complete? Does caution
lessen love?"*

　　　　"Post-Mortem Monologue: Sapphira to Ananias,"
　　　　Megan McDermott

I'd apologize but I'm tired
of opening my mouth only
for you to spit in it. I'd apologize
but given your driving record—
considering the marks
on my neck and back—
looking both ways before crossing
the one-way street of this love
is sensible. I'd apologize
but for you I slaved chords
into the field of my favorite song—
they'll never be free. I'd apologize
but your words have burned
a cross on my lawn and left
me speechless—my lips lacking
moisture, my hands too calloused
shoveling dirt to compose something
meaningful. I'd apologize but
I've run out of raw cheeks
to turn. I'd apologize but I already have.
three times. I'd apologize again but
you wouldn't remember. I'd apologize
but I'm learning self-respect
is like wrestling freedom
from a plantation owner
fallen on hard times. I'd apologize
but I can't trust you
to not Russian doll the moment,
find something even more petty
squeezed inside your hollow shell.
I'd apologize but fuck you.

an open letter to our white friends and supposed allies

you should know: we play a game.
all of us. we imagine the aftermath
of our official lynching—the result
of the inevitable traffic stop, the armed
wrong invasion of our residence, or merely
walking, sitting, sleeping, existing anywhere
a warrant has been issued for our skin-crime.

and so we all hope we will rate a riot.

we count the tweets and t-shirts, the virility
of our # memorials. the number of racist statues
and statutes with nooses around their stone necks.
the number of buildings and cop cars burned
in our name. in all of our names. and knowing
They will attempt to defame the days before our death—
investigate how white our skeletons—
the more competitive among us go the extra mile
to replace your cardboard with Molotov cocktails.

we have scrubbed the earth of all pictures
with do-rags or without diplomas. we consistently
choose church over the club, kale over Kools.
we pre-set our radios to the local NPR affiliate
and give to charity like others daily don clean underwear.
we keep our tox-screens and browser histories as open
and in sight as our hands, to leave no excuse.

and still, we wonder what you will say—
what you will do—when the time comes,
compared to what you are doing right now.

Notes

- None of these poems have anything to do, whatsoever, with my ex-wife. She's pretty great.

- "break-up | | letter | | of resignation" is an erasure poem of a letter composed by _____.

- "*hevel*" – *Hevel* is a Hebrew word most notable for its usage in the book *Ecclesiastes* in the Hebrew Bible. The range of its definitions are contained within the poem.

- "My apples trees will never get across / And eat the cones under his pines . . ." takes its title from Robert Frost's poem "Mending Wall."

- "the reckoning" is a response to a line in Cathy Park Hong's book *Minor Feelings*.

- "fugue state in B minor" employs elements of Robert Frost's poems "Acquainted with the Night" and "Stopping By the Woods On a Snowy Evening."

- "pop quiz for March 19, 2018" responds to the murder of Stephon Clark.

- "never meaning no harm" takes its title from *The Dukes of Hazard Theme Song*.

- "nice white lady" is after Lucille Clifton's poem "white lady."

- "who She is" is after Anne Sexton's poem "The Interrogation Of The Man Of Many Hearts."

- "when asked what it's like to love Her" employs phrases from (roughly in order) Elizabeth Barrett Browning, William Shakespeare, John Fawcett, the Commodores, Martin Sexton, Edna St. Vincent Millay, and the *Song of Solomon* in the Hebrew Bible.

- "jocko graves" employs and references the pseudohistory behind the advent of the Black lawn jockey. Jocko Graves was a fictional slave of George Washington who died holding a lantern and tending to his enslaver's horses, during the famed crossing of the Delaware.

- "the patron saint of suicide" is after Joan Kwon Glass' vastly superior poem "Googling the Patron Saint of Suicides."

- "at some point," like the section epigraphs in the collection, employs phrases from George Saunders' *The Very Persistent Gappers of Frip.*

- "why She be so damn pissed at me all the time" is after Lucille Clifton's poem "why they be mad at me sometimes."

- "when asked how to avoid being seen as racist" is in fact based on a variation on a joke whose origin is unknown, but was once famously told by The Beatles' Paul McCartney.

- "when asked what I learned during the 'community forum' on the appropriateness of my poem" is in response to racists who were (go figure) unhappy with the poem "when asked how to avoid being seen as racist."

Acknowledgments

Grateful acknowledgment to the editors of the following magazines for publishing several of the pieces included here, sometimes in earlier forms:

Bending Genres: "when asked what I learned during the 'community forum' on the appropriateness of my poem"

Cola Literary Review: "the patron saint of suicide"

Discretionary Love: "an open letter to the one who should have got away" & "sweetness"

Fahmidan Journal: "when my colleagues hear our employer confused me with the only other Black teacher in the district"

The Florida Review: "the reckoning"

Frontier Poetry: "an open letter to our white friends and supposed allies"

Identity Theory: "when asked how to avoid being seen as racist"

Jelly Bucket: "My apples trees will never get across / And eat the cones under his pines"

the museum of americana: "'never meaning no harm'"

Nixes Mate Review: "pop quiz for March 19, 2018"

Pangyrus Literature Magazine: "what i learned during Black History Month"

3 Elements Literary Review, "fugue state in B minor

My heartfelt thanks go to the people who have had a hand in the creation of this collection, whether they are aware of it or not: friends and colleagues, I have and haven't met in real life. Alicia Collins, Joan Kwon Glass, Angela Lee, Megan McDermott, Rose J Percy, La Toya Rivers, A.R. Salandy, and Donna Vorreyer.

A special thanks to Allison Blevins and all the good folks at Harbor Editions.

And of course, thanks to _____. For "even though you intended to do me harm, God intended it for the good" (Genesis 50:20). May you find what you're looking for.

Matthew E. Henry (MEH) is the author of *The Third Renunciation* (NYQ Books, 2023), *have you heard the one about...?* (Ghost City Press, 2023), *the Colored page* (Sundress Publications, 2022), *Teaching While Black* (Main Street Rag, 2020) and *Dust & Ashes* (Californios Press, 2020). He is the editor-in-chief of *The Weight Journal*, an associate poetry editor at *Pidgeonholes* and *Rise Up Review*. The 2023 winner of the *Solstice Literary Magazine* Stephen Dunn Prize, MEH's poetry and prose appears or is forthcoming in *Barren Magazine*, *Cola Literary Review*, *Fahmidan Journal*, *The Florida Review*, *Massachusetts Review*, *New York Quarterly*, *Ninth Letter*, *Ploughshares*, *Poetry East*, *Redivder*, *Shenandoah*, *Solstice*, and *Zone 3* among others. MEH's an educator who received his MFA yet continued to spend money he didn't have completing an MA in theology and a PhD in education. You can find him at www.MEHPoeting.com writing about education, race, religion, and burning oppressive systems to the ground.

www.ingramcontent.com/pod-product-compliance
Lightning Source LLC
Chambersburg PA
CBHW020218090426
42734CB00008B/1126